THE OUTDOORS

DUCK HUNTING

by Tom Carpenter

FOCUS READERS

WWW.FOCUSREADERS.COM

Focus Readers is distributed by North Star Editions:
sales@northstareditions.com | 888-417-0195

Produced for Focus Readers by Red Line Editorial.

Photographs ©: Steve Oehlenschlager/iStockphoto, cover, 1, 21; JoMo333/Shutterstock Images, 4–5; J. David Willians/iStockphoto, 6; Suzi Nelson/Shutterstock Images, 8–9; rodimov/Shutterstock Images, 11; Steve Oehlenschlager/Shutterstock Images, 12; shaunl/iStockphoto, 14 (top left); eurobanks/iStockphoto, 14 (top right); Antoni Halim/Shutterstock Images, 14 (bottom left); marekuliasz/iStockphoto, 14 (bottom right); vovashevchuk/iStockphoto, 15 (top left); Kolidzei/Shutterstock Images, 15 (top right); mgkaya/iStockphoto, 15 (bottom left); abadonian/iStockphoto, 15 (bottom right); konstantinks/iStockphoto, 16–17; Vlad Kol/Shutterstock Images, 19; BulentGrp/iStockphoto, 22–23; nwbob/iStockphoto, 25; M. L. Arduengo/iStockphoto, 26–27; muratart/Shutterstock Images, 29

ISBN
978-1-63517-228-7 (hardcover)
978-1-63517-293-5 (paperback)
978-1-63517-423-6 (ebook pdf)
978-1-63517-358-1 (hosted ebook)

Library of Congress Control Number: 2017935869

Printed in the United States of America
Mankato, MN
June, 2017

ABOUT THE AUTHOR

Tom Carpenter is a father, duck hunter, and outdoor writer. He has hunted ducks for more than 45 years, and he has guided many young hunters, including his three sons, to their first duck. Tom grew up hunting wood ducks, mallards, and teal along the Wisconsin River and the creeks that flow into it. He now lives near the shores of Bass Lake, Minnesota, and hunts ducks across America's heartland every fall.

TABLE OF CONTENTS

CHAPTER 1

INTO THE MARSH

You put on your **waders** and step into the marsh to set out your **decoys**. You get out your shotgun, shells, and duck calls. Then you sit in the **blind** and wait for ducks to fly overhead. You start making quacking sounds to attract ducks. Soon a flock of ducks flies past. They twist out of the sky toward your decoys.

A hunting blind helps hunters hide from ducks.

In Europe, hunting for ducks and other birds is often called shooting.

You stand up and pick out a **drake** mallard. You swing your shotgun and squeeze the trigger.

People have hunted ducks for thousands of years. For example, early American Indians created decoys out of reeds and twigs. When ducks came to the decoys, hunters shot the ducks with bows and arrows. They also caught ducks with nets or snares.

When European settlers began moving west across North America, they used guns to hunt ducks. At first they shot ducks only for their families to eat. But hunters started shooting millions of ducks to sell in cities. Duck populations became dangerously low.

By the early 1900s, **conservation** efforts had started. Laws set up specific hunting seasons. People could hunt ducks at only certain times of year. As a result, duck populations began to grow. Today, people enjoy duck hunting in many places around the world.

CHAPTER 2

DECOYS AND DUCK CALLS

Hunters use decoys to attract ducks. Each decoy is attached to a string. A small weight keeps the decoy from floating away. A set of decoys on the water is called a spread. To make a spread seem more realistic, duck hunters blow on duck calls. Each duck call is designed to attract a certain kind of duck.

Wooden decoys are carved to look like different species of ducks.

Duck hunters often carry a variety of calls with them.

Many duck hunters use boats to set out their decoy spreads. Some hunters use flat-bottomed boats. These boats are rigged with motors that can navigate shallow water. Other hunters paddle to their hunting spots with canoes or kayaks.

Hunters often wear waterproof clothes such as waders and hip boots. These items help hunters stay dry while they place decoys on the water. **Camouflage** clothing helps hunters blend in with the area around them. Hunters often use blinds to hide and wait for ducks, too.

Hunters often use boats to get to their hunting locations.

There are two main kinds of ducks to hunt. Puddle ducks swim in shallow waters. They can often be found in marshes, ponds, and river backwaters. Puddle ducks tip their tails up in the air to eat water plants. Mallards, teal, wood ducks, and pintail are puddle ducks.

At approximately 14 inches (36 cm) long, buffleheads are one of the smallest kinds of ducks that people hunt.

Diving ducks live near lakes, rivers, and bays. They dive down in the water to get their food. Diving ducks typically eat plants. But they may also eat fish, clams, or tiny shrimp. Ring-necked ducks, redheads, buffleheads, and canvasbacks are diving ducks.

Many hunters use pump-action shotguns or semiautomatic shotguns.

These guns allow hunters to make rapid follow-up shots if the first shot misses. A duck hunter's shotgun is loaded with shells. These shells contain pellets. The pellets are also called BBs or shot. They spread out in the air when the gun is fired. This gives hunters a better chance of hitting a fast-flying duck.

LEADING A DUCK

Ducks fly quickly. This makes them difficult to hit. Hunters wait for the ducks to come very close before firing. They also swing their guns ahead of the duck before pulling the trigger. This is called leading the duck. Leading helps hunters hit the duck instead of shooting behind it.

DUCK HUNTING SUPPLIES

☐ 1. Decoys

☐ 2. Duck calls

☐ 3. Headlamp

☐ 4. Hunting blind

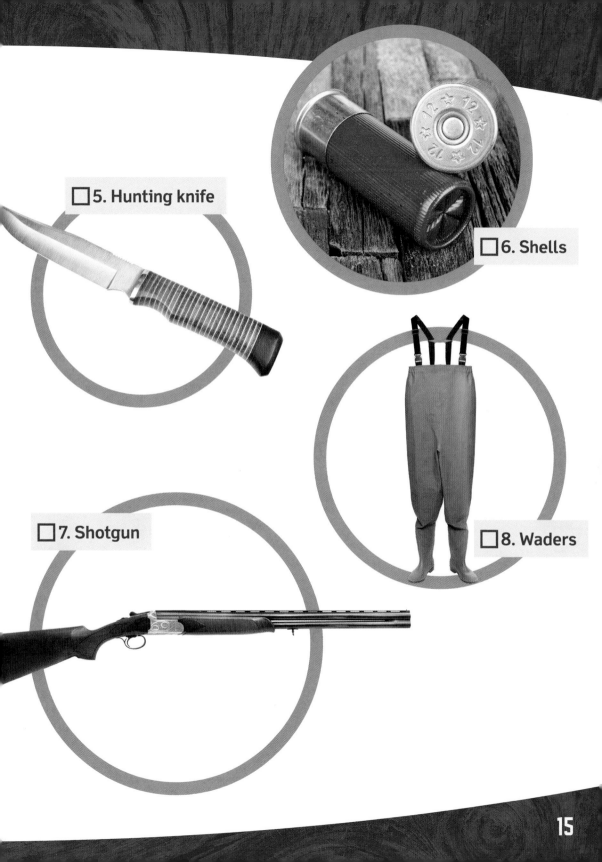

☐ 5. Hunting knife

☐ 6. Shells

☐ 7. Shotgun

☐ 8. Waders

CHAPTER 3

SCOUTING AND HIDING

Scouting is the process of looking for a good hunting spot. When scouting, hunters use binoculars to watch the skies and water. They look for places where ducks are likely to be. Potholes are good hunting spots. These dips in the ground can often be found near large marshes. Many potholes are filled with water.

A swamp or pond can be a good place to find ducks.

Ducks often come to small potholes to escape other hunters.

A U-shaped lake or a **slough** near a river can also be a good hunting spot. Points are good places to find ducks, too. A point is a piece of land that sticks out into a larger body of water. Ducks often have to fly past these places.

Puddle ducks will eat in grain fields. Duck hunters place special decoys in harvested grain fields. Then the hunters hide in small bags or structures known as layout blinds. When ducks fly in, the hunters jump up out and shoot.

All ducks are challenging to hunt because they can see everything as they

Hunters in layout blinds often wear camouflage clothing.

fly over hunters' hideouts. However, ducks tend to land facing into the wind. Smart hunters put the wind at their backs. This allows the hunters to see the ducks coming. The ducks will come in close for a good shot.

When setting out a spread, hunters place the decoys so that incoming ducks have a place to land. An effective decoy spread will have two groups of duck decoys with an opening in the middle. The hunters wait at the opening.

DUCK DOGS

Many duck hunters bring hunting dogs with them. Labrador retrievers, golden retrievers, and Chesapeake Bay retrievers are popular breeds. These dogs swim out into the water and bring back the ducks that hunters have shot. Plus, dogs can help catch ducks that have been hit but are still trying to get away.

Hunting dogs bring ducks back to hunters.

Hunters must hide from the ducks while they wait. Some hunters crouch in vegetation such as cattails, grass, or brush. Others build blinds out of wood. Then they cover the blinds with cattails, reeds, or branches. These blinds often have seats. Some even have heaters and places for hunting dogs to sit.

CHAPTER 4

HUNTING SAFETY

Hunting partners line up side by side to shoot ducks. It is important for hunters to plan where each member of their group will stand. Hunters should also plan where each person will be aiming. Each person should choose a shooting zone. A shooting zone is an area where only that person will shoot.

Hunters should handle guns and ammunition carefully.

Hunters should discuss their shooting zones before the hunt begins.

Duck hunters should also wear life vests when wading in water. Many hunters also wear waders that have quick-release buckles. This allows the hunter to get out of the waders in just a few seconds. That

SAFETY RULES

To avoid accidents, hunters of all ages should always follow four gun-safety rules. First, treat every gun as if it were loaded at all times. Second, always point the muzzle in a safe direction. Third, be sure of the target (and what is beyond it) every time the gun is fired. Fourth, keep fingers outside of the trigger guard until ready to shoot.

Following safety rules around guns helps hunters prevent injuries.

way, the waders will not fill up with water and cause the hunter to drown.

People often go duck hunting in cold or rainy weather. Coats and hats help hunters stay warm. Waterproof gloves help keep their hands warm and dry.

CHAPTER 5

PROTECTING DUCK HABITATS

Each year, governments help set the duck hunting season. The season tells when it is legal to hunt ducks. The season is at a different time each year. That is because it is designed to protect duck populations. Each year, the hunting season changes based on how many ducks are in an area.

Protecting nesting habitats helps ducks have safe places to raise their young.

Duck hunters should hunt only during the correct dates. They should not hunt too many ducks. Instead, they stay within the bag limit. A bag limit is the number of ducks a hunter can shoot in one day.

In some places, each person must also purchase duck stamps before hunting. Money from these purchases is used to **preserve** duck **habitats**.

Hunters can also protect ducks' habitats by using nontoxic shot. When hunters fire shot, some of it falls into the water. Lead is poisonous to ducks and many other animals. Animals that eat lead shot could get sick and die.

The Federal Duck Stamp program has helped preserve more than 5 million acres (2 million hectares) of wetlands.

Nontoxic shot does not contain lead. It is made of steel or other metals. Using nontoxic shot helps ensure that ducks will fill the skies for many years to come.

FOCUS ON
DUCK HUNTING

Write your answers on a separate piece of paper.

1. Write a paragraph describing how hunters can help protect duck habitats.

2. Would you rather hunt puddle ducks or diving ducks? Why?

3. Which type of shotgun shell is poisonous to ducks?
   A. steel
   B. iron
   C. lead

4. Why should hunters discuss shooting zones before the hunt begins?
   A. so that all hunters can have the same shooting zone
   B. so that two hunters do not accidentally choose the same zone
   C. so that each hunting dog can be assigned to its own zone

Answer key on page 32.

GLOSSARY

blind
A hideout in natural vegetation.

camouflage
A pattern that is designed to look like its surroundings.

conservation
The careful protection of plants, animals, and natural resources so they are not lost or wasted.

decoys
Imitation ducks that hunters use to attract real ducks.

drake
A male duck.

habitats
The type of places where plants or animals normally grow or live.

preserve
To protect something so that it does not change.

slough
A wet, muddy place.

waders
Waterproof boots and overalls that a hunter can wear to stay dry when standing in water.

TO LEARN MORE

BOOKS

Carpenter, Tom. *Waterfowl Hunting: Duck, Goose, and More.* Minneapolis: Lerner Publications, 2013.

Lambert, Hines. *Hunting Ducks.* New York: PowerKids Press, 2013.

Omoth, Tyler. *Duck Hunting for Kids.* North Mankato, MN: Capstone Press, 2013.

Pendergast, George. *Duck Hunting.* New York: Gareth Stevens Publishing, 2015.

NOTE TO EDUCATORS

Visit **www.focusreaders.com** to find lesson plans, activities, links, and other resources related to this title.

INDEX

Answer Key: 1. Answers will vary; **2.** Answers will vary; **3.** C; **4.** B